Asian Animals
King Cobras

by Joanne Mattern

Consulting Editor: Gail Saunders-Smith, PhD

Content Consultant: Tanya Dewey, PhD
University of Michigan Museum of Zoology

CAPSTONE PRESS
a capstone imprint

Pebble Plus is published by Capstone Press,
151 Good Counsel Drive, P.O. Box 669, Mankato, Minnesota 56002.
www.capstonepress.com

092009
005618CGS10

Library of Congress Cataloging-in-Publication Data
Mattern, Joanne, 1963–
    King cobras / by Joanne Mattern.
    p. cm. — (Pebble Plus. Asian animals)
    Includes bibliographical references and index.
    Summary: "Simple text and photographs present king cobras, how they look, where they live, and what
they do" — Provided by publisher.
    ISBN 978-1-4296-4029-9 (library binding)
    ISBN 978-1-4296-4847-9 (paperback)
    1. King cobra — Juvenile literature. I. Title. II. Series.
QL666.O64M38 2010
597.96'42 — dc22   2009028646

Editorial Credits
Katy Kudela, editor; Matt Bruning, designer; Svetlana Zhurkin, media researcher; Eric Manske, production specialist

Photo Credits
Alamy/Indiapicture, 13; Corbis/dpa/A3838 Jens Ressing, 9; David Liebman Pink Guppy, 21; Digital Vision, 5;
Dreamstime/Omar Ariff Kamarul Ariffin, 1; Getty Images/National Geographic/Mattias Klum, 7, 17; Getty
Images/Visuals Unlimited/Joe McDonald, 11; Nature Picture Library/Lynn M. Stone, 15; Nature Picture
Library/Michael D. Kern, cover; Nature Picture Library/Rod Williams, 19; Shutterstock/Vivian Fung,
cover (background texture)

Note to Parents and Teachers

The Asian Animals series supports national science standards related to life science.
This book describes and illustrates king cobras. The images support early readers in
understanding the text. The repetition of words and phrases helps early readers learn new
words. This book also introduces early readers to subject-specific vocabulary words, which are
defined in the Glossary section. Early readers may need assistance to read some words and to
use the Table of Contents, Glossary, Read More, Internet Sites, and Index sections of the book.

Table of Contents

Living in Asia

King cobras are the world's longest venomous snakes. Found in Asia, these snakes can grow up to 18 feet (5.5 meters) long.

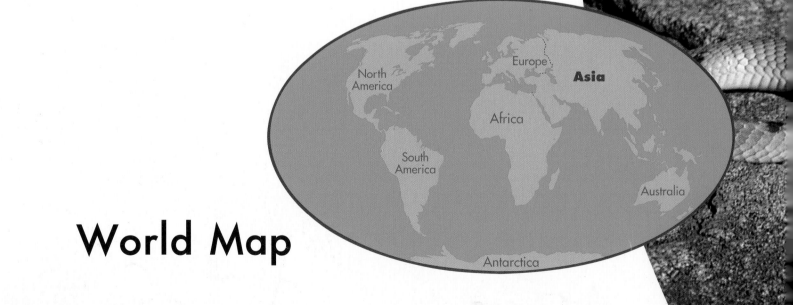

World Map

North America

Europe

Asia

Africa

South America

Australia

Antarctica

King cobras live in southern
and southeastern Asia.
They slither in fields,
rain forests, and swamps.

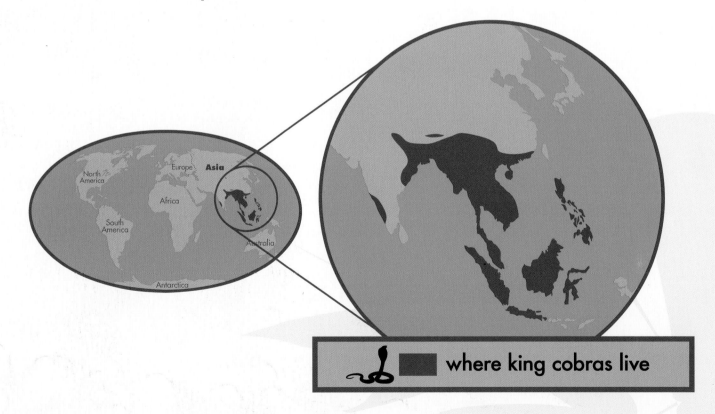

where king cobras live

Up Close!

Smooth green, yellow,

or brown scales cover

a king cobra's body.

The colors help a cobra

blend in with grass and leaves.

King cobras have

strong bodies.

They climb trees and swim.

They can raise their bodies

off the ground.

When in danger,

a king cobra spreads its hood.

The hood makes

the snake look bigger

to scare away predators.

Eating

Strike!

A king cobra bites its prey.

The venom in its fangs

quickly kills the animal.

King cobras swallow
their food whole.
Cobras breathe
through a tube
while swallowing.

Staying Safe

Female king cobras

keep their eggs safe in a nest.

The females guard their eggs

until they hatch.

All king cobras stay watchful.

They look for mongooses

and larger snakes.

They use their fangs

and venom to stay safe.

Glossary

fang — a long, hollow tooth

hatch — to break open

hood — the part of a cobra's neck that can be stretched out to look bigger

mongoose — an animal that has a slender body, a long tail, and brown or black fur

predator — an animal that hunts other animals for food

prey — an animal hunted by another animal for food

rain forest — a thick area of trees where rain falls almost every day

scale — one of the small, hard plates that cover the bodies of fish and reptiles

venom — a poison that some animals make; king cobras are venomous because they produce venom.

Read More

Kudela, Katy R. *The Pebble First Guide to Snakes.* Pebble First Guides. Mankato, Minn.: Capstone Press, 2009.

O'Hare, Ted. *Cobras: Amazing Snakes.* Amazing Snakes. Vero Beach, Fla.: Rourke, 2005.

Wallach, Van. *Cobras.* Snakes. Mankato, Minn.: Capstone Press, 2009.

Internet Sites

FactHound offers a safe, fun way to find Internet sites related to this book. All of the sites on FactHound have been researched by our staff.

Here's all you do:

Visit *www.facthound.com*

FactHound will fetch the best sites for you!

Index

Word Count: 166
Grade: 1
Early-Intervention Level: 18